The Romans

John Malam

PowerKiDS
press.

New York

Published in 2011 by The Rosen Publishing Group Inc.
29 East 21st Street, New York, NY 10010

First Edition

Produced for Wayland by Calcium
Design: Paul Myerscough
Editor: Sarah Eason
Editor for Wayland: Camilla Lloyd
Illustrations: Geoff Ward
Picture Research: Maria Joannou
Consultant: John Malam

Library of Congress Cataloging-in-Publication Data

Malam, John, 1957-
The Romans / by John Malam. — 1st ed.
    p. cm. — (Dig it: history from objects)
ISBN 978-1-4488-3285-9 (library binding)
1. Rome—Civilization—Juvenile literature. 2. Rome—Antiquities—Juvenile
literature. I. Title.
DG78.M35 2011
937—dc22

                                            2010023832

Photographs:
Corbis: The Gallery Collection 14; Dreamstime: Neil Harrison 15b; Fotolia: Ordus
17b, 27c; The Grange Collection/Topfoto: 21t; Photolibrary: Age Fotostock/Russell
Mountford 20, C.M. Dixon 15t, Imagestate 21b; Shutterstock: Dmitry Chernobrov
23b, 26b, Clara 3, 24, Ant Clausen 25b, Alfio Ferlito 5l, 25lt, Javarman 7, 26t,
Mitrofanova 9b, Kenneth V. Pilon 9tl, 26cl, Jens Stolt 9tr, 26cr, Khirman Vladimir
12, 13t, Keith Wheatley 9tc, 26cc; Wayland Picture Library: 11b, 13b, 17t, 18b,
22t, 22b, 27t, 27b; Wikimedia Commons: 6, 10, 23t, Matthias Kabel 19, Remo 8,
Orge Shuklin 4, 16, The Yorck Project/ Zenodot Verlagsgesellschaft mbH 11t, 18t.
Cover photograph: Wikimedia Commons

Contents

Who Were the Romans?

Around 2,000 years ago, different groups of people lived in Italy. One group was called the Latins. They lived in several villages that were all close together. In about 1000 BCE, the villages joined together to form a town, which grew into a city. The city became known as Rome, and its people were called Romans.

Leaders of Ancient Rome

Before the Latins came to power, another group, called the Etruscans, was in charge. The Latins fought with the Etruscans. In 509 BCE, the Latins took over, and the city of Rome was born. Rome was ruled by leaders who were chosen by the Roman people. This system is called a **republic**. The Roman Republic lasted for almost 500 years.

Eventually, the rulers of Rome started to argue. In 27 BCE, one man was chosen to rule Rome. The leader was called an **emperor**. For the next 500 years, Rome was led by emperors.

HUNGRY HORSE
Emperor Caligula loved his racehorse Incitatus so much that he gave him an ivory trough filled with barley and flakes of gold.

Roman artists made sculptures of their emperors from marble. This is a portrait of Augustus, the first Roman emperor.

The Roman Empire

The Romans were powerful. They fought their neighbors and took over all of Italy. Then they took control of land in Europe, North Africa, and the Middle East. The **Roman Empire** formed as more land came under Roman control. The empire covered a vast area and Rome was its capital.

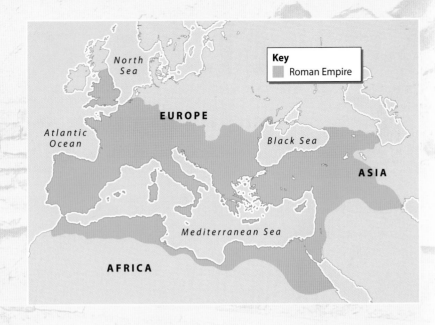

The Roman Empire reached its peak in the early 100s CE. It was divided into areas called provinces, all of which were ruled from Rome.

What Does it Tell Us?

Many Roman sculptures show two boys, Romulus and Remus, being looked after by a wolf. These sculptures celebrate the birth of Rome. Romulus and Remus were twins who were left to die but were later rescued by a wolf that fed them with her milk. The boys grew up to be men and built a city beside the Tiber River. Romulus killed Remus after an argument about who should be its king. Romulus became the first king of the new city. He named it Rome, after himself.

City of Rome

Rome was a magnificent city at the heart of the Roman Empire. The first Roman emperor, Augustus, said this about Rome: "I inherited it brick and left it marble." It was his way of saying he had rebuilt Rome, giving it grand buildings of shiny white stone.

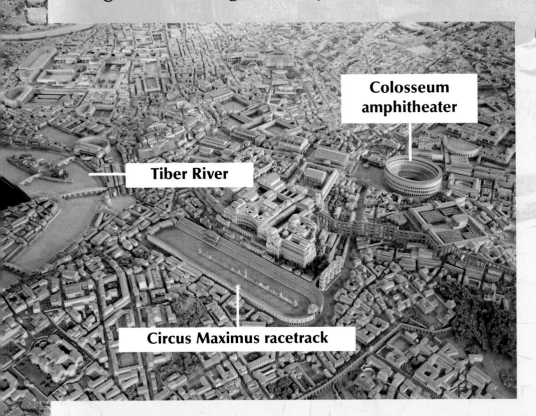

Colosseum amphitheater

Tiber River

Circus Maximus racetrack

A model of Rome, shows the city as it looked in the early 300s CE. It shows the Tiber River, the city streets, and main buildings.

TELLING TIME
Emperor Augustus erected a giant sundial in Rome—the pointer was an ancient statue brought from Egypt.

A Description of Rome

By the early 300s CE, around 1.5 million people were living in Rome. Most Romans were very poor, and they lived in tiny rooms in crowded apartment buildings. Only the rich lived in large townhouses. Around the city were 28 libraries, 11 town squares, 19 aqueducts carrying fresh water, 1,352 water fountains, 11 bathhouses, 856 small bathhouses, 29 main roads, 8 bridges, 2 racetracks, 2 **amphitheaters**, 3 theaters, 36 arches, 290 warehouses, 254 flour mills, and 144 public lavatories.

What Does it Tell Us?

Many people have found Roman coins buried in the ground, so we know the Romans used them to pay for goods and for people's work. The coin with the lowest value was the bronze as (one as would buy a bunch of grapes). A silver denarius was worth 16 asses (15 denarii would buy a pair of men's leather boots). The most valuable of Roman coins was the gold aureus—worth 25 denarii or 400 asses.

The Forum

The city center was the Roman **Forum**, or Great Forum. This huge square was about 330 feet (100 meters) long and 230 feet (70 meters) wide. Public buildings, temples, and shops surrounded the Forum on all sides. The Forum was the center of Rome. Politicians, lawyers, and army generals made their important speeches in the Forum. Moneylenders, food sellers, and pickpockets did their work around the edges of the square.

This picture shows the ruins of the Roman Forum, as they appear today. The Forum was the most important of all the public squares in Rome.

Shopping City

Rome was a city of shops and markets. Every few days, farmers came to the city with fresh fruit and vegetables. They sold their produce from stalls set up along market streets. Other markets were inside market halls, where people went to buy bread, fish, meat, oil, wine, and other everyday household items.

Roman Townhouses

Roman towns were laid out on a grid of streets. The streets were in straight lines and crossed at right angles. Between the streets were squares, where the town's houses, shops, and other buildings stood.

Houses of the Rich

Wealthy Romans had large townhouses with many rooms. Many of them had two floors—an upstairs and a downstairs. Rich Romans had their own bathroom. Poorer Romans had to use the public bathhouses. Walls were painted with bright colors decorated with pictures. Hard-wearing **mosaics** covered the floors.

The townhouse of a rich Roman family was on two levels. It had a courtyard, several rooms, and a garden. Most townhouses were much smaller than this.

Houses for the Middle Class

For better-off Romans, home was a few rooms at the back of the family shop or restaurant. Most shops and restaurants were single-story buildings that faced the street. Customers came and went from the front of the building. The family lived in private rooms at the back. They had bedrooms, a living room, a dining room, and a courtyard where meals were cooked in the open air.

BAD SMELL

Sewage drained into the Tiber River. If the river level rose, the sewage was forced back up into homes that were connected to the drains.

Slums for the Poor

Most Romans who lived in towns were poor. Poor people lived in simple houses or crowded apartment buildings. The tallest buildings were six stories high, rising 70 feet (21 meters) from ground level. Large families were crammed into dark rooms. People in the top rooms were the poorest. Their rooms had no fresh water and no toilets—they had to leave the building for these.

 This wall painting decorated the house of a wealthy Roman. Only the rich could afford to buy a painting like this one.

What Does it Tell Us?

Body scrapers, or **strigils**, have been found in Roman remains. Romans used strigils at the bathhouses. Inside were hot rooms. Steam made people sweat. As they sweated, dirt was forced out of their skin, and they rubbed it off with a strigil. This photograph shows a strigil and an oil container.

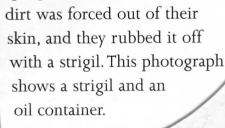

The Countryside

Farming was at the center of Roman life. In the countryside around every Roman town were farms called **villas**. The villas produced food to feed the population. Food that couldn't be produced locally, or was in limited supply, was brought in from other parts of the Roman world.

This mosaic shows a large farmhouse in the countryside.

Farms and Farming

Roman farms could be large or small. A large farm had a lot of land, a big farmhouse, and many people working for the owner. The owner might be a rich man who lived in the nearby town. He hired a manager and slaves to run his farm for him. A small farm was the opposite—a patch of land with a farmhouse for the farmer and his family. Both types of farm grew similar crops and kept similar animals, which they sent to market.

Crops and Farm Animals

Wheat was the most popular crop, and the best farmland was used to grow it. Other crops grown by farmers were barley, beans, cabbages, carrots, celery, onions, garlic, lentils, lettuces, and peas. Fruit crops included apples, figs, grapes, melons, olives, pears, and plums. Cows, goats, and sheep were kept for their meat and milk. Pigs were just for meat. Geese, hens, and pigeons gave eggs and meat. Bees were kept for honey.

 A Roman mosaic shows farm workers stepping on grapes to squeeze out the juice.

What Does it Tell Us?

Archaeologists have found many large pottery storage jars, called **amphorae**. They were used to carry oil and wine from farms to markets. They had pointed bases, so they had to lie on their sides. The liquid inside ran along the neck and touched the bung (lid). The bung was kept wet by the liquid and swelled up in the neck. This stopped the contents from leaking out of the jar.

GARBAGE HEAP
A huge hill found in Rome today, is made from millions of broken amphorae, thrown away when they became empty.

Food and Drinks

Cooking was risky in Roman times because of the danger of fires. For this reason, poor people who lived in crowded apartments in the city of Rome were banned from cooking at home. Instead, they bought their meals at the city's bars and taverns. Only rich Romans cooked at home—in open-air hearths in their courtyards.

A Roman butcher uses a cleaver to chop through a joint of meat.

The Day's Meals

The Romans had little to eat for breakfast. Usually, it was a snack of bread, cheese, and fruit. At lunch time, they might eat more bread and cheese. The main meal was eaten in the afternoon, when the town's takeout restaurants were busy selling spicy sausages and stews. After the savory course, Romans ate fruit, cakes, and pastries.

CHIC CHOW
At one Roman banquet, guests were served with 600 ostrich brains and peas mixed with gold.

Table Manners and Recipes

Mealtimes were messy. Most people ate with their fingers, so they were always washing their hands. Burping and breaking wind were acceptable at the meal table—today, of course, these are bad manners. At a big meal, such as a banquet, some Romans even made themselves throw up, so they had room to eat more food!

What Does it Tell Us?

Many mosaics show wealthy Romans enjoying themselves at lavish banquets. Guests lay on couches on their left sides, propped up on their elbows. In front of them were napkins to catch bits of food. They reached over to a table and took food with their right hands. Many courses were eaten, and the meal could last for hours. Servants brought the food and cleared the dishes, while musicians sang and played instruments.

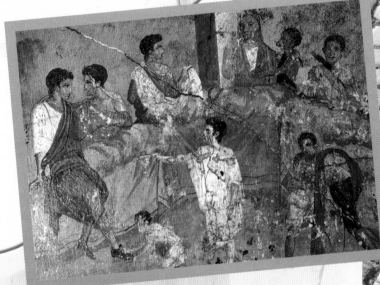

This Roman mosaic shows two squid, which were a favorite food. One Roman recipe uses mashed squid to make rissoles (food rolls), which were then fried and served with fish sauce.

A lot is known about Roman food because many recipes have survived. Many ingredients are still in use by cooks today, but some are not. For example, some Roman recipes used jellyfish, sea urchins, dormice, and flamingos, which people don't eat today.

Clothes and Crafts

We know a lot about Roman clothes and crafts, because there are so many statues, mosaics, and paintings that show what they wore and what their hairstyles were like. Objects found on Roman sites reveal the things that they made and how they made them.

Roman Clothes

For a long time, men from leading Roman families wore a **toga** as the standard item of clothing. The toga was a single piece of cloth wrapped around the body. The women from wealthy families wore a **stola**, which was an ankle-length pleated gown. However, the toga and stola were bulky, so they went out of fashion and were replaced by **tunics**.

Ordinary Romans, working people, country folk, and slaves had always worn easy-to-wear, knee-length tunics, but eventually everyone did. Rich people could afford tunics made of fine cloth. Poor Romans made do with cheap fabric. In cold and wet weather, woolen cloaks with hoods were worn over tunics. In the street, people wore leather sandals or boots. In the house, they put on lightweight sandals or slippers.

A toga was a single piece of cloth wrapped around a man's body, then draped over his left shoulder.

Roman Crafts

Skilled craftspeople produced a huge range of items. Potters worked with clay to make household crockery. Gold and silver were used by jewellers for brooches, rings, chains, and bracelets, as well as expensive bowls, cups, and plates. Artists made magnificent statues from blocks of marble. Mosaic-makers covered floors and walls with little cubes of colored stone to make hard-wearing surfaces.

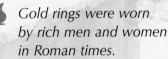

Gold rings were worn by rich men and women in Roman times.

What Does it Tell Us?

Statues and mosaics tell us a lot about Roman fashion. This mosaic shows a hairstyle from about the 100s CE, when it was fashionable for women to wear their hair combed up into a high crest. In later years, women preferred to comb their hair back and tie it in a bun. The woman in this mosaic is also wearing makeup, earrings, and a necklace and bracelet.

children and Schools

Roman children were given their names within a few days of birth. The naming ceremony was a time of celebration. Prayers were said, and babies were given a lucky charm, called a **bulla**, to wear for protection during childhood.

Going to School

Many children never went to school, especially those from poor families. For those who did, school began at the age of seven. One teacher taught them to read and write, and another taught them simple arithmetic. They learned by copying examples and by saying sentences and numbers over and over.

Children would use a writing stylus and wooden writing tablet like the ones the woman in this picture is holding.

What Does it Tell Us?

Children's toys tell us that Roman children had time to play, just like children do today. They had many different toys, including rag dolls, spinning tops, and hoops. Some children had models of chariots, like this bronze one (left). These could be moved along the ground in pretend chariot races.

Boys went to grammar school from the age of about 11 or 12, but girls left school and stayed at home. Boys learned the rules or grammar that governed the Latin language (the language of the Romans). They also learned to read and write Greek, which was the second language of the Roman world.

Boys from wealthy Roman families were taught **oracy**—the art of public speaking. They learned to speak clearly and choose their words carefully—skills they needed for work as lawyers or politicians.

Becoming Adults

A girl was considered an adult when she reached 14 or 15. From then on, she could get married. On her wedding day, she took off the bulla she had worn since childhood. A boy could marry from the age of 14, but he was not considered to be an adult until 16. Only then could he take off his bulla.

This statue shows a Roman girl playing knucklebones. She tosses little bones into the air and catches them on the back of her hand.

IN TROUBLE
A child who misbehaved in class might be lifted onto the shoulders of another pupil, then caned on the backside by the teacher.

Romans and Religion

The Romans believed in many gods. Each god had the power to look after a different part of life. People prayed to the gods and left gifts for them at their temples. In return for pleasing the gods, Romans hoped that they would take care of them in life and the afterlife.

The Main Gods

Some gods were only worshiped in a few places. Others gods were worshiped all over the Roman world. Here are some of them:

The war god Mars was the most important god after Jupiter, the king of the gods. The month of March is named after him.

Diana	Goddess of the moon and hunting
Janus	God of doorways and the New Year
Juno	Queen of the gods; goddess of women and marriage
Jupiter	King of the gods; god of the heavens and weather
Mars	God of war
Mercury	God of communications and travelers
Minerva	Goddess of wisdom
Neptune	God of the sea
Pluto (or Dis)	God of the underworld
Venus	Goddess of love
Vesta	Goddess of fire and the hearth
Vulcan	God of fire and volcanoes

BURNING BRIGHT
Inside the Temple of Vesta in Rome was a sacred fire. It was attended by priestesses, who never let the flames go out.

Roman Temples

Temples were the houses of the gods on Earth. A statue of the god was the most important part of a temple. The Romans believed that the god's spirit lived inside it. The statue faced the front of the temple. When the doors were opened, it "looked" out to the courtyard and watched as people left gifts of food and money. Priests sacrificed animals—the bigger the animal, the greater the gift.

This fresco shows Vulcan hammering a design into a gladiator's helmet.

What Does it Tell Us?

Roman gravestones tell us about the person who died. The inscription usually began with the letters "DM," or the words *Dis manibus*. This is the Latin for "To the gods of the underworld." After this came details about the person—his or her name, where they were from, and how old they were when they died. This is the gravestone of a Roman soldier named Fortunatus, who served with the Third Augustan legion ("LEG III AUG").

Defending Rome

The Romans had a powerful and well-organized army, led by strong generals. The army defended the city of Rome and its frontiers. The army also conquered lands far from Rome, which is how the empire expanded.

How the Roman Army was Organized

From about 70 CE, the Roman army was made up of about 30 large units (**legions**), each commanded by a **legate**. At full strength, a legion had about 5,120 foot soldiers (**legionaries**), divided into ten groups (**cohorts**). The cohorts were split into smaller units (centuries), each with 80 men (at one time it was 100 men).

A **century** was led by a **centurion**. In addition to legionaries, who were Roman **citizens**, the army had foot soldiers known as auxiliaries. They were not Roman citizens. Instead, they were foreigners who had decided to fight on the Romans' side.

🔔 *A legionary's helmet was made from bronze. The back sticks out to protect the soldier's neck.*

ROMANS VS. BRITONS

In 60 CE, an army of 100,000 Britons, led by the warrior queen Boudicca, wiped out the Roman IXth Legion.

🔔 *This special type of helmet, with a face mask, was worn by an officer during parades or displays by the army.*

Weapons and Armor

Roman legionaries were given a dagger (**pugio**), a short sword (**gladius**), and a javelin (**pilum**). They wore strips of metal and leather armor on their bodies. Helmets protected their heads, cheeks, and necks. Shields protected them from enemy missiles, and by overlapping shields above their heads, a group of soldiers formed a **testudo**, or tortoise shape. It gave the men protection and allowed them to advance toward the enemy. For long-distance fighting, catapults fired big arrows with iron tips, and other machines hurled rocks.

 Roman soldiers protect themselves with their shields in a testudo (tortoise) formation.

What Does it Tell Us?

Hadrian's Wall in Britain is 73 miles (117 kilometers) long. It shows us the northernmost boundary of the Roman Empire. Hadrian's Wall was a stone and turf wall built around 122–128 CE on the orders of Emperor Hadrian (reigned 117–138 CE). Along its length were fortified gateways, turrets, and forts, each housing between 500 and 1,000 troops. Beyond the wall were tribes that the Romans called **barbarians**.

Entertainment

The Romans had time to enjoy themselves during the many public holidays throughout the year. They might watch a play or go to the games to see animal hunting, chariot racing, and **gladiators** fighting.

The Theater

Plays were acted out in the afternoon in open-air theaters in the shape of a semicircle. There were two main types of plays—comedies, which were funny, and tragedies, which were serious. Actors wore clothes of different colors depending on who they were supposed to be—white for the elderly, purple for the rich, and red for the poor.

A retiarius ("net-fighter") was a gladiator who fought with a net, a three-pronged trident, and a long dagger.

The Racetrack

Thousands of people went to the **circus**, or racetrack, to watch the chariots race. The track was narrow, and crashes were common when the chariots turned at each end. The biggest racetrack in Rome was the Circus Maximus. Teams of charioteers did seven laps at up to 46 mph (75 km/h). It took about ten minutes to cover a lap of 3.2 miles (5.2 kilometers).

EAT ASH
A Roman writer claimed gladiators ate ash from fires. He said it was to increase their strength.

What Does it Tell Us?

Actors, who were all men, wore masks with exaggerated features. The audience knew what part the actor was playing from the mask—a happy mask for a comedy and a sad mask for a tragedy. A tragedy mask is shown on the left. A brown-colored mask showed the actor was playing the part of a man. A white mask was for a woman.

The Amphitheater

The grandest entertainment was held at the amphitheater—an open-air building that was either oval or round. Tickets were free, and those lucky enough to get one enjoyed a day's events. In the morning, wild animals were sent into the arena, where hunters killed them. At noon, criminals were put to death by wild animals. In the afternoon, gladiators fought each other. If both men fought well, the crowd might let them live. A man who fought badly could be killed by his opponent. The crowd shouted, jeered, and clapped, and loved every minute of it.

The Colosseum was Rome's largest amphitheater with room for about 50,000 spectators.

Quiz

1. **What would you see at the amphitheater?**
   a. Actors
   b. Gladiators
   c. Gods

2. **What was a bulla?**
   a. A lucky charm worn only by boys
   b. A lucky charm worn only by girls
   c. A lucky charm worn by boys and girls

3. **What were the names of the twins fed by the wolf?**
   a. Remulus and Romus
   b. Romules and Remos
   c. Romulus and Remus

4. **Who wore a stola?**
   a. A child
   b. A man
   c. A woman

5. **How tall were the tallest apartment buildings in Rome?**
   a. 5 stories high
   b. 6 stories high
   c. 7 stories high

6. **Who is the Roman god of the sea?**
   a. Mars
   b. Jupiter
   c. Neptune

7. **What was the main crop grown by Roman farmers?**
   a. Barley
   b. Wheat
   c. Oats

8. **What did soldiers put over their heads to make a testudo formation?**
   a. Their shields
   b. Their helmets
   c. Their swords

9. **What was the Roman Forum?**
   a. The center of Rome
   b. A theater in Rome
   c. A Roman temple

10. **What time of day was the main meal eaten?**
    a. Late morning
    b. Late afternoon
    c. Late evening

ANSWERS

1. b.
2. c.
3. c.
4. c.
5. b.
6. c.
7. b.
8. a.
9. a.
10. b.

Timeline

c. 1000 BCE	A group of villages joins together to form a town, which later became the city of Rome.
753 BCE	According to legend, this was the year Rome was founded.
c. 753–509 BCE	The city of Rome was ruled by kings, who were very unpopular.
509 BCE	The last king was overthrown, and the Roman Republic began.
264 BCE	The first gladiatorial contest was staged in Rome.
264–146 BCE	The Romans fought wars against Carthage, a city in North Africa, which they won.
214–146 BCE	The Romans fought wars against Greece, which they won.
59–51 BCE	The Romans fought wars against Gaul (France and Belgium), which they won.
45 BCE	General Julius Caesar became the dictator (sole ruler) of Rome.
44 BCE	Julius Caesar was assassinated because it was believed he had too much power.
27 BCE	The Roman Republic ended. Augustus became the first Roman emperor, and the Roman Empire began.
43 CE	The Romans invaded Britain.
60 CE	Queen Boudicca led a rebellion in Britain against the Roman invaders.
64 CE	Much of Rome was destroyed by a fire.
79 CE	Several Roman towns in Italy, including Pompeii and Herculaneum, were destroyed when the volcano Vesuvius erupted.
80 CE	The Colosseum—the largest amphitheater in Rome—was opened.
120 CE	The Roman Empire reached its greatest extent.
120–28 CE	Hadrian's Wall was built in Britain.
284 CE	The Roman Empire was divided into the East and the West.
313 CE	Christianity and all other religions were accepted throughout the Roman Empire.
330 CE	Constantinople replaced Rome as the capital of the Roman world.
c. 404 CE	The last known gladiatorial contest was staged at the Colosseum.
410 CE	The city of Rome was invaded by barbarians.
476 CE	Romulus Augustulus, the last emperor of the Western Empire, abdicated (left the throne). The Roman Empire in the west ended.
476–1453 CE	The Eastern Empire flourished for 1,000 years, until Constantinople was conquered by the Turks.

Glossary

amphitheater An open-air building in which shows were performed.

amphora (plural: amphorae) A large pot for storing oil, sauce, or wine.

barbarian A person from outside the Roman world.

bulla A lucky charm worn by children.

centurion The commander of a company (century) of legionaries.

century A company of 80–100 soldiers.

circus A racetrack for horse-drawn chariots.

citizen A man born in Rome. Citizens had to obey Roman laws.

cohort A unit of 480 soldiers in a legion.

emperor The ruler of the Roman world.

Forum The square in the center of a Roman town.

gladiator A highly trained fighter, named after his main weapon, the gladius.

gladius A short sword used by a gladiator.

legate The commanding officer of a legion.

legion A division of 4,000 to 6,000 soldiers.

legionaries The soldiers belonging to a legion.

mosaic A picture usually made of small stone cubes.

oracy The art of speaking in public.

pilum A javelin used by Roman soldiers.

pugio A dagger used by Roman soldiers.

republic A state or country governed by officials elected by the people.

Roman Empire All the areas ruled by Rome.

stola The main garment worn by women.

strigil A scraper used to clean the body.

testudo A "tortoise" formation of soldiers.

toga The main garment worn by men.

tunic A knee-length garment, like a long shirt.

villa A large house with farm buildings in the country.

Further Information

Books

How People Lived in Ancient Rome
by Jane Bingham
(PowerKids Press, 2008)

How the Ancient Romans Lived
by Anita Ganeri
(Gareth Stevens Publishing, 2010)

The Ancient Romans
by Allison Lassieur
(Children's Press, 2005)

Web Sites

Due to the changing nature of Internet links, PowerKids Press has developed an online list of Web sites related to the subject of this book. This site is updated regularly. Please use this link to access this list:
http://www.powerkidslinks.com/dig/romans

Index